Your Psychic Connection

Matthew & Leitreanna Brown

"The intuitive mind is a sacred gift, and the rational mind is a faithful servant. We have created a society that honors the servant and has forgotten the gift."

— *Albert Einstein*

"There is a universal, intelligent, life force that exists within everyone and everything. It resides within each one of us as a deep wisdom, an inner knowing."

— *Shakti Gawain*

"Everyone is born with psychic abilities. It is just a matter of learning how to access and use them."

— *Edgar Cayce*

"There is no matter as such—what we consider as matter arises from a force that brings particles into vibration and holds them together."

— *Max Planck*, Father of Quantum Physics

"The day science begins to study non-physical phenomena; it will make more progress in one decade than in all the previous centuries of its existence."

— *Nikola Tesla*

Copyright © 2023 by Leitreanna Brown.

All rights reserved.

No part of this publication may be reproduced, stored in a retrieval system, or transmitted in any form or by any means, electronic, mechanical, photocopying, recording,

scanning, or otherwise, without the author's prior written permission.

Limit of Liability/Disclaimer of Warranty: This publication provides accurate and authoritative information regarding the subject matter covered. We sell it with the understanding that neither the author nor the publisher is engaged in rendering legal, investment, accounting, or other professional services. While the publisher and author have used their best efforts in preparing this book, they make no representations or warranties concerning the accuracy or completeness of the book's contents and expressly disclaim any implied warranties of merchantability or fitness for a particular purpose. Sales representatives may create or extend no warranty or written sales materials. The advice and strategies contained herein may not be suitable for your situation. You should consult with a professional when appropriate. Neither the publisher nor the author shall be liable for any loss of profit or any other commercial damages, including but not limited to special, incidental, consequential, personal, or other damages.

Your Psychic Connection.

By Leitreanna Brown,

Cover design by Leitreanna Brown

Edited and formatted by VAPBooks,

VAPBooks Publishing, Virginia, USA.

Table of Contents

Dedication 6

Acknowledgment 7

Unlocking the Ancient Power Within 9

Welcome 10

The Truth Behind Psychic Ability 12

How the Mind Manifests Psychic Insights 17

Why Understanding Your Psychic Messages Matters 21

The Ten Core Psychic Abilities 22

Unlocking the Clairs 26

How the Brain Senses "Beyond the Five Senses." 28

The Importance of Exercising the Psychic Mind with Divination Tools 48

Deepening Understanding and Connection 51

Oracle Card Reading 52

Psychic Lesson 64

Tea Leaf Reading– Psychic Exercise 71

The Art of Co-Creation with the Universe—Manifesting . 84

Step-by-Step Guide to Psychic Manifesting 87

Psychic Manifesting Journal 93

Astral Projection 98

Astral Projection 105

Aura Reading 109

The Psychic Mindset 116
Trust the Journey Within 118
Conclusion 120

Dedication

To every reader who finds a piece of themselves within these chapters, take to heart that every word written is to be a treasure map to help you discover the psychic talents already within you.

Acknowledgment

To Dr. Bob Taylor

Thank you for truly listening to me when I was just a young student, uncertain but curious. You saw something in me—even before I fully understood it myself—and you began gently testing and challenging my psychic abilities as soon as you recognized my potential. You never treated me like just a kid. Instead, you saw a young person with a mind eager to explore, and you helped guide that exploration with respect and encouragement. I am deeply grateful for the way you helped me understand what I was capable of. Your strength and courage inspired me and still does.

To Linda Williams

Thank you for the many years of teaching, guiding, and loving. Your energy techniques did not just expand my knowledge—they transformed my life. Truly, you saved me. Through your open-hearted methods, I learned how to let energy flow through me in ways that changed how I see the world. What began as a psychic ability deepened into a spiritual understanding—one rooted in connection with our Creator and the sacred energy that exists in all things.

You taught me how to see, feel, hear, and embrace the divine presence within everything and everyone. You helped me rise to the next level of my journey, always teaching with love and generosity—not only to me, but also to my husband, Matthew. I love you deeply, and I am forever thankful for the light you have brought into our lives.

Unlocking the Ancient Power Within

Psychic abilities are not a modern invention; they are as old as humanity itself. For thousands of years, across every continent and culture, seers, oracles, shamans, and visionaries have served as spiritual beacons. Tribes relied on them not only to protect their people but to guide hunters to game, locate water, foresee dangers, and interpret the will of nature and spirit alike. Their visions saved lives, guided migrations, crowned leaders, and even changed the course of history.

From the revered traditional healers and women of the First Nations—experts in remote viewing and astral travel—to the famed Oracles of Delphi, whose words determined the fate of empires, the psychic thread weaves through every chapter of our human story. Ancient scriptures honor prophets like Joseph, whose dreams swayed kings, while mystics like Nostradamus glimpsed distant futures with eerie clarity. Even Homer, through poetry, offered cryptic warnings of destiny unfolding.

These were not just tales or superstition, they were early acknowledgments of the mind's untapped potential and humanity's innate connection to something greater.

Welcome

In this book, we will explore the rich legacy of psychic ability and bring its wisdom into the present day. You will uncover the foundations of intuitive development and be introduced to practical tools like oracle cards, tea leaf reading, egg divination, manifesting, aura reading, and more. Along the way, you will learn to sense energy and tap into the deep intuitive knowing that already lives within you.

Psychic ability is not about magic spells or mysticism, it is about energy, awareness, and the sacred power of intuition. It is about turning into the quiet wisdom of your soul and learning to trust what your inner voice has always known: you already hold the key.

This is more than just a book. It is an invitation to journey inward, to awaken your intuitive gifts, and to reconnect with the unseen world around you.

"Prayer is telephoning to God, and intuition is God telephoning to you." — Florence Scovel Shinn, *The Magic Path of Intuition*

NOTES

What do you expect to gain from reading this book?

Do you suspect that you have a type (or types) of psychic ability?

Do you have methods for increasing your psychic abilities?

"Psychic abilities aren't just about seeing the future, they're about reclaiming your inner power, trusting your intuition, and changing the course of your life by listening to the wisdom within."—Leitreanna Brown

The Truth Behind Psychic Ability

Science, Spirit, and the Mind's Hidden Power

When many people hear the word "psychic," images from movies or television often come to mind—characters draped in velvet, layered in bangles, peering into crystal balls from candlelit corners. These portrayals, while entertaining, do little justice to the profound reality of psychic phenomena. The truth is far more grounded—and far more extraordinary.

Every human being possesses psychic potential. It is not the domain of the eccentric or the mystical elite, but rather a natural extension of human consciousness. The human brain remains one of the greatest frontiers of modern science. Vast regions of it remain unexplored, functioning in ways we do not yet fully understand. When we observe individuals recovering from brain injuries and re-learning vital tasks through different neural pathways, we witness firsthand the brain's remarkable adaptability—and its hidden depths.

One particular area of the brain has drawn the attention of mystics and scientists alike: the pineal gland. Often referred to as the *third eye*, this small, light-sensitive gland is nestled deep within the center of the brain. It is responsible for producing melatonin and regulating our circadian rhythms, but mystics and philosophers have long believed it does much more. To many individuals, it functions as the bridge between the physical and spiritual dimensions—a conduit to enhanced consciousness.

The 17th-century philosopher René Descartes famously declared the pineal gland to be the *seat of the soul*. Descartes, a mathematician, scientist, and metaphysical thinker, believed it was the point at which the immaterial soul interacted with the physical body. This idea became the cornerstone of what is now known as Cartesian Dualism, and it inspired centuries of inquiry into the nature of consciousness.

Later thinkers, such as Geoffrey Jefferson, echoed Descartes' assertions, referring to the pineal gland as the *notal point* of spiritual cognition. Though science continues to investigate the gland's physical functions, its reputation as the seat of psychic vision remains deeply rooted in both metaphysical tradition and experiential evidence.

Psychic ability, then, is not supernatural, it is **extra-natural**. It is a deeper expression of the energy that moves through all things. Just as scientists can measure electrical activity in the brain using electrodes, so, too, can we begin to understand that energy itself is at the heart of consciousness. Everything in existence is made up of atoms, and within every atom, electrons dance in rapid motion. This energy, this life force, is the spiritual foundation of existence.

From this perspective, we come to understand ancient teachings like Reiki in a new light. Derived from the Japanese words *Rei* (universal consciousness) and *Ki* (life energy), Reiki is the practice of channeling conscious life force energy for healing, protection, and revelation. Through intention, we direct energy. Through awareness, we receive wisdom.

It is this awareness—the ability to sense, interpret, and interact with unseen forces—that lies at the heart of psychic development. Divination practices such as tarot, oracle cards, tea leaves, egg reading, and palmistry are all tools that help us tune into the subtle energies around us. They are not magical in themselves; rather, they are mirrors reflecting the truths already present within us.

The intention you bring to these tools shapes the message you receive. As many experienced readers believe, the power behind divination is not external. It comes from the client's own energy, the wisdom of their higher self, and the universal consciousness that connects us all.

As psychic medium Anthon St. Maarten wisely stated:

"Psychic and paranormal phenomena will always be a source of controversy because it is an inconvenient reminder that there is more to our reality than meets the eye."

And further:

"I have always disliked the term 'paranormal' because it refers to anomalies — 'abnormal' phenomena not yet understood by science… I am no longer willing to consider my psychic abilities to be an 'unfortunate anomaly.'" — Anthon St. Maarten, The Sensible Psychic

Reflection:

- Were you surprised to learn that as early as the 1600s, philosophers were investigating the physical source of psychic awareness?

- Do you now see how energy is in all things—and how, by connecting to it, your own intuitive power may increase?

- Are you beginning to feel the stirrings of your own psychic potential?

If so, you are right where you need to be. This journey is just beginning.

How the Mind Manifests Psychic Insights

From a Whisper to a Hurricane

Psychic information often arrives in subtle, mysterious ways, sometimes barely noticeable, like a gentle kiss of air, and other times as powerful and overwhelming as a hurricane. Understanding this spectrum of experience is crucial to recognizing and trusting your psychic abilities.

The Whisper:

Subtle Psychic Impressions

At times, psychic messages are quiet and fleeting, like a soft breeze brushing your skin or a brief, unexplained feeling in your gut. These subtle nudges might be a quick flash of insight, a sudden sense of knowing, or a delicate emotional impression. They are often easy to dismiss or overlook because they do not demand immediate attention. But these quiet moments can be just as important as louder experiences.

These whispers come from the subconscious mind tapping into the quantum field of information—a vast, interconnected web of universal knowledge beyond time and space. The mind processes countless signals beneath the surface, and the faintest impressions may emerge into consciousness as gentle intuitive nudges.

The Hurricane:

Intense Psychic Experiences

Other times, psychic notions crash into your awareness like a hurricane — intense, vivid, and impossible to ignore. These might manifest as powerful emotions, vivid mental images, sudden physical sensations, or an overwhelming sense of certainty. During these moments, your intuitive "antenna" is fully tuned, and information floods in from the subconscious or spiritual realms.

These powerful waves often arise during times of emotional upheaval, meditation, or deep focus. They demand your attention because the message they carry is urgent or profoundly significant.

The Spectrum:

Learning Your Psychic Language

The key to developing your psychic abilities is learning to recognize the unique way your mind delivers these messages—whether as whispers or hurricanes. Everyone experiences psychic notions differently, and even for one person, the intensity can vary from moment to moment.

- Pay close attention to the feelings, images, or thoughts that arise without explanation.

- Notice the physical sensations: a flutter in your chest, a tingling on your skin, or a sudden chill.

- Observe the emotional tone: Is it calming or urgent? Peaceful or stirring?

- Track your inner symbols: What recurring shapes, colors, or words appear in your mind?

Building Confidence and Translation Skills

Like learning a new language, the psychic realm uses symbols, feelings, notions, and knowing as its vocabulary. Developing psychic skills means building a dictionary for yourself, a personal symbolic language that turns elusive impressions into concrete knowledge.

- Confidence grows when you learn to trust your experiences, even if they seem strange or fleeting at first.

- Practice helps you separate psychic impressions from everyday thoughts and fears.

- Journaling your experiences trains your mind to recognize patterns and meanings.

- Validation comes from seeing how your intuitions align with actual events or outcomes.

Why Understanding Your Psychic Messages Matters

Without clarity about how your psychic information arrives, you risk doubting yourself or ignoring important insights. But when you know your unique psychic language and trust your internal signals, your intuitive mind becomes a powerful guide.

The process is much like turning on a radio: at first, the signals might be fuzzy and inconsistent. But with patience and attention, your psychic receiver sharpens, allowing you to discern even the faintest whispers—or navigate the wildest hurricanes—with confidence and grace.

Psychic notions manifest on a spectrum, from gentle nudges to overwhelming storms. By learning how your mind sends these signals and by trusting your feelings, symbols, and inner knowing, you develop the confidence to translate psychic impressions into meaningful knowledge, unlocking the true power of your intuition.

The Ten Core Psychic Abilities

Unlocking the Mysteries of Your Intuition and Soul Energy

The universe whispers to us in many languages—through feelings, visions, sounds, and knowing beyond logic. These core psychic abilities are the channels through which cosmic communication flows. Everyone has the seeds of these gifts within them. Developing them is less about "scoring points" and more about awakening to the subtle signals your soul and mind are already sending you.

1. Clairsentience—The Gift of Intuitive Feeling

To be clairsentient is to feel the invisible currents of energy around you. Like a living antenna, you pick up emotions, moods, or histories embedded in places and people. Psychometry—the ability to hold an object and sense its past—is a classic example. Science tells us that human skin is richly supplied with nerve endings and bioelectric signals, making it a prime receptor for subtle energetic cues.

"The body never lies—it's the first psychic instrument we have." — Jayne Ann Krentz

2. Clairaudience—The Art of Intuitive Hearing

Clairaudience means "clear hearing" of messages beyond the physical realm. You might hear whispers from spirit guides, ancestral voices, or melodies that seem to float from nowhere. These experiences, often mistaken for "hearing voices," are neurologically linked to auditory processing centers of the brain reacting to non-physical stimuli.

"Psychic hearing is not madness; it is the music of the universe waiting to be understood." -Matthew and Leitreanna Brown

3. Clairvoyance—The Power of Intuitive Seeing

To be clairvoyant is to witness "pictures in the mind" or visions like watching a silent movie. These images arise from the brain's occipital lobe but are filtered through the subconscious mind, which taps into the collective unconscious concept first explored by Carl Jung. Visionary experiences are often spontaneous but can be trained and refined.

"I can only gaze with wonder and awe at the depths of our psychic nature." — Carl Jung

4. Claircognizance—The Knowing Beyond Knowing

Claircognizance delivers instant "downloads" of insight—answers arriving without logical deduction. Modern neuroscience reveals that intuition operates through rapid, unconscious processing of stored knowledge and sensory data, giving the brain lightning-fast gut responses.

"Intuition is always listening; all you have to do is ask."
— mindbodygreen.com

5. ESP (Extra-Sensory Perception)—Perception Beyond the Five Senses

ESP is the umbrella for all psychic sensing beyond sight, sound, touch, taste, and smell. It includes telepathy, remote viewing, and precognition. Rigorous studies at Stanford

Research Institute in the 1970s (under Russell Targ and Harold Puthoff) demonstrated statistically significant psychic phenomena that intrigued government agencies like the CIA and NASA—confirming the reality of ESP in controlled environments.

"The results were worth the investment: psychic ability exists and can be harnessed." — Russell Targ

6. Telepathy—Mind-to-Mind Communication

The science of telepathy suggests that brainwaves and quantum entanglement may allow thoughts to cross physical space without words or signals. People with strong telepathic gifts can sense others' emotions or thoughts directly. This ancient skill, rediscovered and validated through modern experiments, reveals the profound connectivity of consciousness.

"The mind has no boundaries except those we impose. When one mind touches another without words, that is where true understanding lives." — Dr. Leitreanna Brown.

Unlocking the Clairs

Discovering Your Psychic Voice Through Divination

Everyone has a psychic sense—it is simply a matter of understanding how your intuitive "voice" speaks. Psychic abilities are often grouped into the **Clairs**, or "clear" senses, which mirror our physical ones but operate on a spiritual level:

- **Clairvoyance**—"Clear seeing": You receive messages through mental images or visions.

- **Clairaudience**—"Clear hearing": You hear messages, sounds, or words from the spirit realm or higher self.

- **Clairsentience**—"Clear feeling": You sense energy, emotions, or physical sensations tied to people or places.

- **Claircognizance**—"Clear knowing": You just *know* something without knowing how—you receive sudden insights or truths.

- **Clairalience**—"Clear smelling": You perceive scents with no physical source, often tied to spirit messages.

- **Clairgustance**—"Clear tasting": You experience tastes that offer intuitive clues or spirit communication.

Divination tools—like tarot cards, pendulums, tea leaves, or runes—act like tuning forks for your intuition. They create a sacred space for your psychic senses to activate and express themselves.

As you use these tools, you will notice how your psychic type shows up:

- Do you *see* vivid imagery while reading tarot? You may be clairvoyant.

- Do you *feel* a strong emotional reaction when holding a pendulum? That is clairsentience.

- Do you *hear* an inner voice during an oracle card draw? Clairaudience is speaking.

Divination not only sharpens your skills, it teaches you your psychic language. With practice, your natural gift becomes clearer, stronger, and deeply personal.

How the Brain Senses "Beyond the Five Senses."

1. The Brain as an Electromagnetic Receiver

The brain is not just a processing unit; it is an electromagnetic organ that emits and receives frequencies. Our neurons communicate via electrical impulses, which create measurable electromagnetic fields. Some scientists, like those involved in the Stargate Project (a U.S. military remote viewing program), have theorized that the brain can tune into information like a radio receiver—noticing vibrations, thoughts, or images that exist outside ordinary awareness.

"The brain is a frequency decoder. It does not create consciousness—it receives it." — Adapted from theories by neurobiologist Dr. Karl Pribram and physicist David Bohm.

2. The Role of the Pineal Gland (The "Third Eye")

Deep within the brain lies the pineal gland, often associated with psychic and mystical insight. It is sensitive to light and governs circadian rhythms, but it also contains photoreceptor cells similar to those in the eyes. Ancient traditions and modern metaphysical thought consider this the seat of clairvoyance or "inner sight."

"The pineal gland is the principal seat of the soul."

— *René Descartes*

3. Subconscious Pattern Recognition

Our brains constantly process vast amounts of sensory data—even if we are not consciously aware of it. Through the subconscious mind, we can detect emotional energy, atmospheric changes, and even the intentions of others, which may register as a gut feeling, a sudden knowing (claircognizance), or a subtle inner nudge.

- These feelings may arrive gently, like a breeze ("a kiss of air"), or forcefully, like a hurricane of realization—especially in moments of heightened emotional or psychic sensitivity. Many times, people have extreme psychic notions when their lives are in danger.

4. Mirror Neurons and Empathic Perception

Mirror Neurons and the Psychic Gift of Clairsentience

Mirror neurons are a fascinating feature of the human brain—specialized cells that activate both when we perform an action and when we observe someone else performing that same action. These neurons are thought to be the biological basis for empathy, enabling us to instinctively understand and "feel into" the experiences of others. This built-in neurological system allows us to sense emotional states such as sadness, joy, or fear just by witnessing another person's facial expressions, body language, or tone of voice.

While traditionally studied within the realms of neuroscience and psychology, some theorists and spiritual practitioners believe that mirror neurons may also be the scientific key to understanding certain psychic abilities—particularly *clairsentience*.

What Is Clairsentience?

Clairsentience, or "clear feeling," is the psychic ability to perceive emotions, energy patterns, or physical sensations that originate outside oneself. This ability is closely linked with what many refer to as being an *empath*—someone who not only notices but feels the emotional and energetic states of others, often deeply and intuitively.

Imagine walking into a room and instantly sensing tension without anyone speaking or brushing past a stranger and suddenly feeling overwhelmed with sadness or joy that you know isn't your own. These are signs of clairsentience at work. It is like reaching out in the darkness and unexpectedly grabbing someone's hand—you can't see them, but you *know* they are there because you feel their presence so clearly.

The Empath's Challenge: Discernment

While this ability can be profound and healing, it also requires discernment—the ability to separate your own feelings from those you are absorbing from others. Without boundaries, empathic individuals can become overwhelmed, mistaking others' grief, anxiety, or excitement as their own and experiencing emotional fatigue or confusion.

Developing clairsentience includes:

- **Grounding** regularly to stabilize your own energy.
- **Energy clearing** practices like breathwork, visualization, or salt baths.

- **Journaling** emotions to track what feels foreign or unusually intense.

- **Setting energetic boundaries**, such as imagining a protective light or shield.

Mirror Neurons as a Psychic Bridge

The theory is that mirror neurons may function as a neurological conduit for this type of energetic information. Just as they help us understand a friend's pain or joy through observation, they might also be the brain's way of interpreting subtle energetic cues that we are not consciously aware of—vibrations, emotional waves, or physical sensations transmitted through the energy field.

This would mean clairsentience is not merely intuitive but possibly hard-wired—a natural psychic extension of our biological capacity to connect. The exploration of quantum consciousness reflects ideas from the Orch OR theory proposed by Stuart Hameroff and Roger Penrose, which suggests that consciousness arises from quantum processes within brain microtubules. For a deeper understanding of mirror neurons, please refer to their research.

Whether viewed through the lens of science or spirit, clairsentience invites us to reconnect with our emotional intelligence on a soul-deep level. It reminds us that our sensitivity is not a weakness, but a strength—a finely tuned compass that guides us through unseen realms of human and energetic experience. With practice, protection, and presence, clairsentient abilities can become a powerful tool for healing, guidance, and deep empathy.

5. Quantum Consciousness

Some physicists and neuroscientists (like Sir Roger Penrose and Dr. Stuart Hameroff) propose that consciousness may arise from quantum processes in the brain. These processes could enable the mind to access non-local information—knowledge not bound by space or time.

Quantum Consciousness: Bridging Science and Spirit

Quantum consciousness is a fascinating and complex theory that proposes a link between quantum physics and the nature of consciousness—suggesting that our thoughts, awareness, and even psychic abilities might originate or be influenced at the quantum level.

While traditional science has yet to fully explain consciousness, and quantum consciousness remains a theory rather than a proven model, it has inspired deep conversations among physicists, neuroscientists, and spiritual thinkers alike. At its core, *quantum consciousness* suggests that our mind and awareness may be tied to the quantum field—the invisible layer of reality where particles can exist in multiple states at once, communicate instantly over great distances (entanglement), and appear to "choose" a state only when observed (the observer effect). Obviously, astral projection and remote viewing are exercises of quantum consciousness.

This theory implies that:

- Consciousness is not confined to the brain.
- Awareness might be non-local—existing beyond time, space, or physical boundaries.
- Our thoughts, intentions, and awareness may interact with the quantum field, influencing matter and reality itself.

Key Ideas Associated with Quantum Consciousness

1. The Observer Effect

In quantum physics, particles behave like waves of potential until they are observed—at which point they "collapse" into a single, concrete state. Some theorists interpret this to mean that the consciousness shapes reality. Your awareness, then, may play a role in manifesting outcomes, connecting this concept with psychic manifestation and intention-setting.

2. Quantum Entanglement

Entangled particles affect each other instantly, no matter how far apart they are. This echoes how psychic phenomena such as telepathy, remote viewing, or spiritual connection can happen across great distances without physical interaction.

3. Non-Local Consciousness

Some scientists, like Stuart Hameroff and Roger Penrose, suggest that consciousness arises from quantum-level processes within the microtubules of brain cells. According to their *Orch-OR theory* (Orchestrated Objective Reduction), consciousness is not a byproduct of the brain alone, but a fundamental part of the universe, possibly tapping into a deeper quantum reality that connects all living things.

How This Relates to Psychic Development

If consciousness exists at the quantum level, then psychic abilities might be natural expressions of how we interact with that field. This would mean:

- **Remote viewing** taps into non-local awareness.
- **Telepathy** uses quantum entanglement between minds.
- **Manifestation** focuses thought into quantum possibility, guiding reality to take form.
- **Clairvoyance or precognition** could involve accessing quantum information beyond linear time.

Implications for You

Understanding or even contemplating quantum consciousness can expand your psychic practice by:

- Encouraging you to trust your inner knowing, even when it defies logic or time.
- Helping you feel more interconnected with others and the universe.

- Reinforcing your intentions and awareness are powerful tools that shape your experiences.

Quantum consciousness does not replace spiritual understanding, it enriches it. Whether you are meditating, practicing remote viewing, or setting intentions for healing, you are participating in a deeper, energetic language that quantum theory may be just beginning to describe. As science evolves, the mysteries of the soul and the universe may prove to be more connected than we ever imagined.

Decoding the Psychic Brain

Every thought, feeling, and intuitive insight you receive is communicated through a unique, symbolic language your brain uses to transmit psychic information. This language is not spoken in words but in images, feelings, symbols, and subtle impressions—each carrying meaning beyond the limits of ordinary logic.

Understanding this psychic language is essential because it allows you to decode the messages your subconscious and spirit send you. It helps you distinguish genuine psychic insights from ordinary thoughts or emotions and opens the door to deeper self-awareness and spiritual growth.

By learning to recognize and interpret these symbols, you gain access to a powerful internal guidance system—one that can reveal hidden truths, warn of dangers, and illuminate your path in ways no external advice can. Mastering this language transforms psychic experiences from confusing or fleeting moments into clear, actionable knowledge, empowering you to navigate your life with confidence and clarity.

Developing Psychic Sensory Language

To understand and trust these subtle messages, you must learn how your own brain processes non-physical data:

- Do you see images in your mind's eye (clairvoyance)?
- Do you feel sensations or energy shifts (clairsentience)?
- Do you just know things instantly (claircognizance)?

- Do you hear thoughts, tones, or voices (clairaudience)?

"Psychic impressions speak in the language of symbol, emotion, and sudden knowing. The more you trust and track these impressions, the clearer they become."

Our brains often communicate psychic information through **symbols and images** that carry emotional and spiritual significance rather than literal meanings. These symbols act like a secret code, transmitting messages from the subconscious, spirit guides, or loved ones in the spirit realm. Because these messages come from an intuitive, non-linear source, they are often expressed as familiar objects, colors, sounds, or sensations that resonate with specific meanings unique to you or shared across cultures.

For example, when you see flowers in a psychic vision, dream, or spontaneous image, this can symbolize a spirit's awareness of an upcoming celebration or milestone. It is like the spirit is saying, "I see your joy, I'm present, and I celebrate with you."

Flowers carry universal associations of beauty, growth, and happiness, making them ideal for conveying positive, congratulatory messages from the other side.

By meditating, journaling, and practicing divination, you begin to notice how these impressions show up in your mind. Over time, you will recognize when a whisper of spirit is calling—whether it is a soft kiss of intuition or a roaring gust of insight. The first step to understanding your mind's messages is to clear your mind and connect with universal energy. I recommend using guided meditation (Awakening the Quantum Mind) and practicing your symbol discovery. See below for steps on how to conduct these self exercises.

Guided Meditation: *Awakening the Quantum Mind*

Purpose:

To quiet the conscious mind, open the subconscious gateways, and connect with the universal intelligence — the quantum field — where psychic insights arise.

Find a quiet space and sit comfortably. Close your eyes and take a deep breath in… and slowly breathe out.

Begin by feeling your body relax with each breath. Notice your feet on the ground, your spine straight but relaxed.

Now, imagine a soft, radiant light glowing at the center of your forehead — your "third eye," the seat of intuition and inner knowing.

As you breathe in, feel this light grow brighter and warmer. With each exhale, release any distracting thoughts or worries. Picture them dissolving like mist.

Know that your brain generates about 70,000 thoughts each day — but for now, you only need to focus on the light and your breath.

Visualize this light extending beyond your body, expanding into a vast, infinite field — the quantum mind or unified field of consciousness. This is the source of all knowing, connecting everything in the universe — and you are a part of it.

Say quietly to yourself:

"I open my mind and heart to the wisdom of the universe. I am calm. I am connected. I receive."

Feel yourself tuning in like a radio receiver, allowing insights, feelings, or images to flow in naturally.

There is no need to force anything. If a thought, image, or feeling arises, simply observe it without judgment.

Rest here for a few minutes, breathing gently, open to the mystery and science merging into your awareness.

When you are ready, gently bring your attention back to your body, wiggle your fingers and toes, and open your eyes.

Note: As you study the connections between quantum physics and psychic abilities are speculative and not widely accepted in the scientific community.

Psychic Exercise: *Symbol Discovery*

Purpose:

To build trust in your psychic senses by interpreting symbols that emerge from your subconscious, blending intuition with mindful observation.

Materials Needed:

- A deck of simple symbol cards (you can make your own: draw or print shapes like circles, triangles, waves, stars, eyes, spirals, trees, etc.)
- A quiet space and a journal or notebook

- A pen or pencil

Step 1: Centering

Sit quietly and do the guided meditation above or simply close your eyes and take five deep breaths to calm your mind.

Step 2: Shuffle & Draw

Shuffle your symbol cards with the intention: *"Show me the symbol that holds a message for my highest good."*

Draw one card without looking.

Step 3: Observe & Feel

Look at the symbol. Do not rush to analyze it. Instead, breathe and notice:

- What feelings arise in your body?
- What memories, images, or thoughts come to mind?
- What colors, shapes, or patterns stand out?

Step 4: Write Your Intuitive Message

In your journal, write down:

- The symbol's description.
- Your immediate impressions or feelings.
- Any insights or guidance that comes through — even if they seem unclear or strange.

Step 5: Reflect

Ask yourself quietly:

"How does this symbol relate to my life right now? What is it trying to teach me?"

Write any additional thoughts.

Step 6: Science & Mystery Connection

Remember: your brain's subconscious mind is using stored memories, sensory impressions, and subtle energy cues to create this symbol and its meaning. This is your intuition at work — a fascinating interplay between neural processes and the deeper quantum consciousness.

Closing

Thank the universe and your inner self for the guidance. Close your cards and take a few grounding breaths.

Guided Meditation: *Awakening the Quantum Mind*

Purpose:

To quiet the conscious mind, open the subconscious gateways, and connect with the universal intelligence — the quantum field — where psychic insights arise.

Find a quiet space and sit comfortably. Close your eyes and take a deep breath in… and slowly breathe out.

Begin by feeling your body relax with each breath. Notice your feet on the ground, your spine straight but relaxed.

Now, imagine a soft, radiant light glowing at the center of your forehead — your "third eye," the seat of intuition and inner knowing.

As you breathe in, feel this light grow brighter and warmer. With each exhale, release any distracting thoughts or worries. Picture them dissolving like mist.

Know that your brain generates about 70,000 thoughts each day — but for now, you only need to focus on the light and your breath.

Visualize this light extending beyond your body, expanding into a vast, infinite field — the quantum mind or unified field of consciousness. This is the source of all knowing, connecting everything in the universe — and you are a part of it.

Say quietly to yourself:

"I open my mind and heart to the wisdom of the universe. I am calm. I am connected. I receive."

Feel yourself tuning in like a radio receiver, allowing insights, feelings, or images to flow in naturally.

There is no need to force anything. If a thought, image, or feeling arises, simply observe it without judgment.

Rest here for a few minutes, breathing gently, open to the mystery and science merging into your awareness.

When you are ready, gently bring your attention back to your body, wiggle your fingers and toes, and open your eyes.

Remember: your brain's subconscious mind is using stored memories, sensory impressions, and subtle energy cues to create this symbol and its meaning. This is your intuition at work — a fascinating interplay between neural processes and the deeper quantum consciousness.

The Importance of Exercising the Psychic Mind with Divination Tools

Developing psychic abilities is much like training any other skill. The more you practice, the stronger and clearer your connection becomes. Divination tools such as tarot cards, pendulums, runes, crystal balls, or oracle decks function as psychic training instruments that help you focus, interpret, and refine your intuitive senses.

How Divination Tools Help You Hone Your Psychic Type

Each person's psychic gifts are unique—some may be naturally clairvoyant (seeing), others clairaudient (hearing), or clairsentient (feeling). Divination tools provide a structured yet flexible framework that allows you to:

- **Focus your intuition:** The symbols and patterns in these tools serve as anchors, helping your mind zero in on psychic impressions and reduce mental noise.

- **Clarify your psychic signals:** When you draw a tarot card or watch the pendulum's movement, you translate subtle psychic nudges into tangible insights, making it easier to recognize and trust your intuitive hits.

- **Practice interpretation:** Divination requires decoding symbolic language, sharpening your ability to understand psychic messages from yourself, spirits, or the universe.

- **Receive feedback:** Using tools regularly allows you to evaluate your interpretations against real outcomes, helping you learn what resonates and improving your accuracy.

Regular use of divination tools trains your brain to tune into higher frequencies of information:

- **Expands awareness:** Tools open you up to messages from your subconscious, spirit guides, or energetic fields you might otherwise overlook.

- **Strengthens concentration:** Focusing on cards or pendulum swings boosts your mental discipline, crucial for psychic clarity.

- **Builds confidence:** Seeing your psychic insights manifest or confirming guidance builds trust in your abilities, reducing doubt and fear.

- **Encourages mindfulness:** The ritual of using divination tools invites you into a quiet, receptive state where psychic impressions flow more freely.

Deepening Understanding and Connection

Beyond sharpening skills, divination tools deepen your relationship with your psychic self and the unseen world. They become mirrors reflecting your inner wisdom, helping you recognize patterns, cycles, and spiritual lessons. Over time, they teach you that psychic information is never random—it carries meaning tailored to your journey.

In essence, these tools are more than just props—they are psychic coaches, translators, and companions guiding you step-by-step toward greater intuitive mastery.

Oracle Card Reading
A Step-by-Step Exercise to Strengthen Your Psychic Abilities

Oracle cards are powerful tools for developing your intuition and tuning into universal energy. Think of this exercise as psychic training—a way to stretch your inner knowing, connect with subtle energies, and build confidence in your spiritual insight. There are no rigid rules in the world of oracle readings—only intention, presence, and openness.

Before You Begin: Understand the Theory

Divination cards, such as tarot or oracle decks, are not magical in themselves. They work as mirrors—tools that reflect your inner wisdom and energetic truth. They help you tune into your subconscious, the energies around you, and even your connection with Spirit.

Here is a clear, mystical-yet-grounded step-by-step guide for using oracle cards to exercise your psychic muscles suitable for your book or journal-style activity section:

Oracle Card Reading: A Step-by-Step Exercise to Strengthen Your Psychic Abilities

Oracle cards are powerful tools for developing your intuition and tuning into universal energy. Think of this exercise as psychic training—a way to stretch your inner knowing, connect with subtle energies, and build confidence in your spiritual insight. There are no rigid rules in the world of oracle readings—only intention, presence, and openness.

Before You Begin: Understand the Theory

Divination cards, such as tarot or oracle decks, are not magical in themselves. They work as mirrors—tools that reflect your inner wisdom and energetic truth. They help you tune into your subconscious, the energies around you, and even your connection with Spirit.

LAB ACTIVITY: Strengthening Your Psychic Intuition with Oracle Cards

Step 1: Choose Your Deck

Select an oracle or tarot deck that calls to you. Let your intuition guide you—whether it is Angel Oracle, Raven Tarot, Witch's Brew, or any deck that stirs your curiosity. If you are drawn to a deck's artwork, theme, or energy, trust that it is meant for you.

Tip: It's believed your deck becomes attuned to you and your energy. Over time, your readings will deepen as your connection with the cards grows.

Step 2: Set the Scene

Create a quiet, sacred space. Light a candle, burn incense, or play soft music, whatever helps you feel grounded and open. Clear your mind and center yourself with a few deep breaths.

Step 3: Invite a Partner (Optional)

Ask a classmate, friend, or partner to volunteer for a reading. Have them sit quietly and focus on a question they would like insight into. The question can be general ("What do I need to know right now?") or specific.

Step 4: Shuffle and Separate

Hold the deck in your hands and focus on the energy of your question or your partner's question. As you shuffle, think or say aloud: "What does [client's name] need to know right now?"

Once shuffled, invite your partner to separate the deck into three stacks, then restack them in the order they feel is right.

Step 5: Draw and Interpret the Cards

Draw the cards according to the deck's instructions (this might be a single card, a three-card spread, or something more detailed). Take your time to study each card's image, words, or symbols.

Now, allow your intuition to speak. Don't just read from the guidebook—what *feeling, thought,* or *inner nudge* do you get when you see the card? Share that insight with your partner.

Step 6: Reflect Together

After the reading, talk with your partner. Did the message resonate? Was it relevant or helpful to their question? Do not worry about being "right"—the goal is to develop trust in your impressions and learn from the experience.

Step 7: Repeat and Record

Repeat this exercise **at least seven times**, either with different people or over several days. Keep a journal of your impressions, what cards came up, what you sensed, and how your clients responded. Look for patterns or repeated messages.

Step 8: Evaluate Your Progress

After multiple readings, reflect:

- Do you feel more attuned to the cards?
- Are your interpretations becoming more intuitive?
- Do your clients report meaningful experiences?
- Do you feel your psychic awareness is becoming stronger?

Remember...

- Oracle cards are tools—*you* are the channel.
- Your intention and energy shape every reading.
- There are no wrong answers, just lessons, symbols, and messages to explore.
- Practice, trust, and openness are key to psychic growth.

When you tune into your intuition, you begin to speak the language of the soul.

Psychic Training Worksheet: Oracle Card Reading Practice

Session Number: _____

Date: _____

Client Name (or Self-Reading):

_____

Question/Focus for the Reading:

What is the question the reading is focused on?

Deck Used:

☐ Angel Oracle

☐ Raven Tarot

☐ Witch's Brew Tarot

☐ Other: _____

Preparation Notes:

Describe how you prepared for the reading — setting, mood, tools used, breathing, intention, etc.

Card Spread Used:

☐ 1-Card Pull

☐ 3-Card Spread (Past, Present, Future)

☐ Custom/Other:

Cards Drawn & Interpretations

Card Name	Initial Feeling/Intuition	Symbol/Message Interpretation
1.		
2.		
3.		

Write what you felt immediately after pulling each card before consulting a guidebook. Then write a deeper interpretation using intuition and symbolism.

Include as many thoughts and feelings as possible.

Did the Reading Resonate?

☐ Yes

☐ Somewhat

☐ No

Feedback or Client Response:

Psychic Reflection & Growth

1. **Did I feel connected to the cards today?**

   ☐ Strongly

   ☐ Somewhat

   ☐ Not at all

2. **Did I receive any intuitive nudges or images?**

   ☐ Yes

   ☐ No

   (Describe them if applicable):

3. **What could I do differently next time to improve connection or accuracy?**

Key Takeaways from This Session:

(Insights, patterns, emotional reactions, or psychic impressions worth noting.)

"Intuition is seeing with the soul."—*Dean Koontz.*
Track your growth. Trust the process. The more you use your abilities, the stronger they become.

Takeaway from Your Oracle Card Exercise

This oracle card exercise has gently guided you to connect with your inner wisdom and the subtle energies around you. The readings you gave are a personalized message designed to illuminate your path, provide insight, or offer encouragement. Remember, the meaning you felt most strongly during the reading is often the most important—your intuition is your best interpreter.

Through this exercise, you have practiced the art of listening to psychic symbols and trusting your intuitive impressions. Each reading is an opportunity to build confidence, clarity, and a stronger bond with your higher self and spiritual guides.

Self-Reflection Questions

- What was my first impression or feeling when I saw the card?
- Which symbols, colors, or words stood out to me, and why?
- How does the card's message relate to my current life situation or challenges?
- Did any emotions or memories surface while interpreting the card?
- What guidance or action does the card inspire me to take?
- How did using my intuition in this exercise feel—easy, challenging, surprising?
- What have I learned about my psychic language and symbols through this reading?

Journaling your answers will deepen your understanding of both the card's message and your evolving psychic abilities.

NOTES:

Psychic Lesson
Egg Readings (Oomancy)—The Sacred Art of Energy & Symbol

Introduction: The Egg as a Mystic Mirror

Since the time of the ancients, the egg has been a symbol of creation, life, and the mysterious unseen. The Greeks practiced *Oomancy*, reading the whites of eggs for signs and guidance. The Egyptians regarded eggs as sacred, holding the mysteries of rebirth and the eternal cycle of life.

In spiritual work today, the egg is still honored, not as food, but as a sponge for energy, a mirror for your soul, and a mystical tool of cleansing and clarity.

What is an Egg Reading?

Egg readings (or egg cleansings) are a form of spiritual divination where an egg is rubbed over the body to absorb energy and then cracked into water to reveal hidden spiritual patterns.

Unlike tarot or runes, an egg reading is not about the future, it is about your current energetic state, emotional blocks, and spiritual environment.

What You'll Need:

- 1 Raw egg (organic or from a trusted source)
- 1 Clear glass or bowl of water (room temperature)
- Sea salt
- Lemon juice
- A white candle
- Incense (optional)
- Notebook or journal
- Peaceful space

Ritual Preparation

1. Create Sacred Space
    - Light your white candle.
    - Place salt in a circle around the candle.

- Burn incense (sandalwood, frankincense, or lavender work well).

2. Cleanse the Egg

    - Mix salt and lemon juice in water.
    - Gently wash the egg while saying a cleansing prayer or affirmation.

        "May this egg be pure and sacred, a vessel of truth and energy."

    - Rinse and pat dry.

The Psychic Cleansing Ritual

1. Set Your Intention

    - Hold the egg with both hands.
    - Close your eyes, breathe deeply, and speak your intention aloud.

"With this egg, I cleanse all that no longer serves me." "Reveal what is hidden in my energy."

2. Perform the Cleansing

- Slowly rub the egg over your entire body from head to toe.
- Focus on emotional centers: the heart, the back of the neck, your hands, your gut.
- Imagine the egg absorbing negativity and energy blockages.

3. Crack the Egg

- Gently crack the egg into a glass of water.
- Let it settle for 1–3 minutes.
- Do not stir.

Interpreting the Signs

Use your intuition and the guide below to read the spiritual message:

Symbol	**Meaning**
Bubbles around the yolk	Exhaustion, spiritual burnout—rest is needed.

Symbol	Meaning
Faces or animals	Hidden influences: a person or situation affecting you.
Pointed yolk	A curse or intense negative influence.
Dark yolk	The evil eye or spiritual interference.
Yolk sinking down	Repressed emotions or lingering grief.
Cloudy yolk	Emotional confusion, stress, or depression.
Blood in yolk	Immensely powerful black magic—seek spiritual help.
Flower shapes	Blessings and protection. A good sign!
Discolored egg white	Insecurity, blocked confidence.
Egg breaks beforehand	High spiritual interference—cleansing is urgently needed.

Transform & Release

- Add salt to the egg-water mix and flush it down in the toilet.
- Say: "I release this energy. I call in light, peace, and renewal."

Journal Reflection (Mystical Prompts)

- What images or feelings came up as you performed your reading?
- Did any shape, bubble, or movement stand out to you?
- What emotional response did you have when interpreting your egg?
- Did you feel any shift in energy afterward?

Energy Reset Tips (Aftercare)

1. Positive Sound: Play healing music or nature sounds.
2. Light Up Your Space: Use white candles, salt lamps, or soft lighting.

3. Smell the Change: Use incense or essential oils like sage, cedar, or rose.

4. Spiritual Bath: Bathe in sea salt and lavender to seal in the cleanse.

Final Thought

"Eggs are portals of the unseen—vessels through which energy is both held and released. In your hands, they become keys to your own sacred knowing."

– Your Psychic Connection, Second Edition, Leitreanna Brown

Tea Leaf Reading– Psychic Exercise

Psychic Development Exercise using Tea Leaf Readings, designed to feel mystical, accessible, and meaningful to both beginner and intermediate students. It explains the deeper purpose of the ritual and how it can strengthen intuitive skills while also offering practical, magical instructions.

Psychic Exercise: Reading the Leaves—Unlocking Intuition Through Tasseography

"There is truth in the leaves… if your heart is willing to see it."—Old European Proverb.

Why This Exercise Strengthens Psychic Ability

Reading tea leaves, also known as **Tasseography**, is one of the most ancient and poetic forms of intuitive divination. It trains the mind to look beyond the obvious, to **see stories in symbols**, and to **trust spontaneous impressions**.

This form of psychic reading:

- Activates your *clairvoyance* (clear seeing) by spotting images and forms.

- Engages your *clairsentience* (clear feeling) through interpreting intuitive impressions.

- Strengthens your *intuitive imagination*, encouraging the soul to speak symbolically.

- Teaches patience and self-trust as you develop your personal symbol lexicon.

Materials You will Need:

- A wide-mouthed teacup (preferably white or light colored inside)

- A matching saucer

- Loose-leaf tea (black or green are best; avoid overly thick herbs)

- A kettle of hot water

- A quiet and sacred space

- A notebook and pen

The Ritual

1. Prepare the Tea with Intention

- Set a calming atmosphere: candlelight, soft music, and incense, if you like.
- As you boil the water, hold the intention: "Reveal what needs to be known."

Place about one teaspoon of loose-leaf tea into the cup—do not use a strainer—and pour the hot water over the leaves. Let it steep for a moment.

Avoid milk or honey, as they cause the leaves to clump.

2. Drink & Swirl

- The *sitter* (person receiving the reading) slowly drinks the tea until there is only a tablespoon of liquid remaining.
- While sipping, encourage the sitter to focus silently on a question or life situation they would like clarity on.
- After the last sip, the sitter gently swirls the remaining liquid three times in a clockwise motion.
- Invert the cup over the saucer and let it sit for about 30 seconds.

3. Reveal & Read

Turn the cup upright and begin the reading.

Use this guide to decode timing:

Position in Cup	Timing
½ inch from rim	4–5 years out
Mid-cup	2–3 years
Near bottom	In the coming months
Very bottom (center base)	Immediate situation

Common Symbol Meanings

Until you form your own psychic dictionary, use:

Symbol	Meaning
Heart	New love, healing, or reconciliation
Snake	Hidden danger, gossip, or betrayal
Circle	Completion, unity, spiritual wholeness

Symbol   Meaning

Ladder   Promotion, spiritual ascension

Tree   Long life, family roots, or spiritual growth

Bird   News, messages from spirit, freedom

Crown   Achievement, power, honor

Butterfly Transformation, rebirth, inner freedom

Horse   Travel, strength, progress

Cross   Challenges, destiny, divine purpose

Encourage students to feel into the image, not just define it. For example:

"Does the bird look like it is flying or perched? What direction is it facing? What do you feel it wants to say?"

Exercise Tips for Psychic Growth

- **Trust your first impression**–often the true psychic message.

- **Let symbols speak**–do not rush into logic; feel what the shape reminds you of.

- **Do not force it**–if nothing is clear, move on to another part of the cup.
- **Journal what you see**–over time, you will notice personal patterns in your readings.
- **Practice on others**–the more sitters you read for, the more your psychic vocabulary deepens.

Reflection Prompts

After each reading, invite your students to reflect:

1. What symbols stood out the most to you?
2. What feeling or memory did they spark?
3. Did any part of the reading surprise you?
4. How did the sitter respond—what insights did they gain?
5. Did you feel more connected to your inner vision?

Final Thought

"Tea leaf reading teaches us to slow down and *see the invisible.* In a world of noise, it brings us back to symbol, silence, and soul. Every leaf carries a whisper from your intuition—you only need to look."

Here is a clean, easy-to-use Tea Leaf Reading Worksheet formatted for journaling and intuitive practice. You can print or use digitally for your psychic development exercises:

Tea Leaf Reading Worksheet

Date: _____

Sitter (if applicable): _____

Type of Tea:

Question or Focus:

Here are some samples (check one or write your own):

- "I ask this egg to absorb and reveal any energy that is not serving my highest good."
- "With this reading, I seek clarity and truth regarding my current spiritual path."
- "I am open to receive insight about what needs to be healed within and around me."
-

Preparation & Intention

- What ritual or intention did you set before reading?

CHECK ONE OR WRITE YOUR OWN:

- Releasing negative energy or spiritual attachments
- Understanding the source of emotional or physical blocks
- Gaining clarity about a situation, relationship, or decision
- Seeking a spiritual diagnosis for unease or bad luck

REMEMBER TO:

Hold the egg in your hands and imagine light flowing into it from your heart, your third eye, or the universe above. Say your intention again while focusing this energy into the egg. This aligns the egg with your request and activates it as a spiritual tool.

Reading Observations

Location Cup	Symbols Seen	Your Interpretation/Meaning
Near rim (4-5 years out)		
Middle (2-3 years out)		

Lower side (Near future)		
Bottom (Immediate events)		

Intuitive Impressions

- Which symbol or shape stood out the most? Why? How did the image reveal itself to you?

- What feelings, thoughts, or messages did you get during the reading?

- Did any patterns or themes emerge?

Reflection

- How did the reading resonate with you or the sitter?

- What did you learn about your intuition or psychic ability today?

New Symbols & Meanings (Add to your personal dictionary)

Symbol:	Meaning:
Symbol:	Meaning:

Symbol:	Meaning:
Symbol:	Meaning:
Symbol	Meaning

Confidence & Clarity Rating

Takeaway from Your Tea Leaf Reading

As you sat quietly with your cup, the gentle ritual of sipping tea and turning inward allowed your psychic senses to awaken. The act itself—intentional, slow, and mindful—created a sacred space for spirit and intuition to speak.

When you turned the cup, your eyes may have been drawn to certain clumps or streaks of leaves that seemed to form deliberate shapes. These were not just random configurations, they were symbols shaped by energy, reflective of your current emotional and spiritual state.

Perhaps you saw a heart nestled at the base of the cup—immediately evoking a sense of comfort, healing, or even longing. You may have felt warmth, like a subtle pulse in your chest, or the soft presence of a loved one watching over you. This heart might signal a new relationship, a rising self-love, or a reminder from spirit that you are never alone.

You might have seen a ladder climbing up the side of the cup, bringing with it a surge of determination or excitement. Maybe you felt a tightening in your gut or a rush of energy, your body telling you that a breakthrough or a major goal is within reach. Spiritually, this could be a sign of elevation—of climbing not only toward success, but toward deeper understanding.

A bird in flight near the rim may have appeared delicate and fleeting, yet carried with it an unmistakable message of freedom. If you felt lightness or relief, it could mean release from a burden. If the bird felt more watchful, it could be a spirit guide keeping close.

Throughout the reading, notice not just what you *saw*, but what you *felt*. Were there subtle shifts in your emotions, flashes of memory, or an image that appeared in your mind's eye even before looking into the cup? These are psychic impressions, part of your intuitive language.

Self-Reflection Questions for Your Tea Leaf Reading

- What shapes or symbols stood out most in the cup?
- What were my first emotional or physical reactions when I saw each symbol?

- Did any memories or names surface during the reading?

- How do the symbols connect to my current life circumstances or questions?

- Were the feelings I experienced familiar or unexpected?

- Did I hear any inner words or phrases while looking into the cup?

- What message do I feel spirit or my higher self was trying to communicate?

By allowing yourself to see beyond the leaves and into your client's soul or your soul's reflection, you have opened the door to deeper insight. Tea leaf reading is more than fortune-telling—it is a gentle conversation with your intuition, where symbols meet sensation, and where stillness reveals the answers that are already within you.

The Art of Co-Creation with the Universe—Manifesting

What if your thoughts were not just fleeting ideas—but divine codes, pulsing with energetic intent, capable of shaping the very threads of reality?

Psychic manifesting is the sacred art of creation through spiritual alignment, intuitive clarity, and energetic mastery. It reaches beyond traditional manifestation by activating your innate supernatural abilities, your psychic senses, your soul's wisdom, and your connection to the invisible realms.

This practice is not about wishing, it is about *witnessing* the unseen, *feeling* your desires as if they have already happened, and *moving* in harmony with the vibrational truth of what you are calling in.

At its heart, psychic manifesting reveals this universal truth:

"You are not merely a receiver of reality—you are a transmitter."

When you consciously attune your thoughts to your psychic senses—like clairvoyance, clairsentience, and telepathy—

you begin to broadcast your desires into the energetic field of creation. You align with the timelines that already hold your dreams fulfilled, and you speak to the Universe in its native language: frequency.

You are not commanding the future; you are co-creating it—with trust, presence, and profound spiritual precision.

In the pages ahead, you will:

- Discover the *energetic mechanics* behind psychic manifestation.
- Learn to *communicate* with your higher self and spirit guides.
- Practice *emotionally charged visualization* that radiates vibrational intent.
- Create *rituals and symbolic tools* that bridge the spiritual and physical planes.
- Shift from passive hope to empowered co-creation.

Whether you seek love, healing, protection, abundance, or purpose—your psychic gifts are your most powerful instruments.

So, light your candle. Breathe into your heart. Feeling the veil between thought and form begin to thin.

"Your thoughts are not wishes—they are blueprints. When aligned with intention and energy, they become reality."
— Dr. Leitreanna Brown

Your manifestation journey starts now.

Step-by-Step Guide to Psychic Manifesting

Step 1: Clarify Your Desire—(Energetic Mechanics Engage)

Speak your desire clearly to the Universe. Write it in the present tense, as if it already lives in your reality. "I am surrounded by loving relationships that uplift and nourish me."

Step 2: Activate Your Psychic Senses—(Beginning your communication with the universe)

Enter a meditative state. Use clairvoyance (see), clairsentience (feel), or clairaudience (hear) to sense your reality as already here. "What does this outcome feel like in my energy body?"

Be specific. Do you need more sleep? Do you want to improve your health? Feel, see, hear, and experience your energy within your body in a meditative state.

Step 3: Call in Divine Allies (get divine help which increases your emotionally charged visualizations)

Invite your spirit team—ancestors, guides, angels, saints—to co-create with you.

Affirmation: *"I welcome divine guidance and support in this sacred creation."*

Step 4: Elevate Your Frequency (Steps 4 & 5 continue to increase your emotionally charged visualizations)

Feel the joy of already having what you desire. Engage in rituals or actions that anchor this feeling now—dancing, prayer, creativity.

Your emotion is the magnet.

Step 5: Visualize with Psychic Precision

See your outcome in vivid, multi-sensory detail. Place your hand on your third eye to enhance focus.

Feel it. Smell it. Hear it. Embody it.

Step 6: Anchor It in the Physical World - Create rituals and symbolic tools that bridge the spiritual and physical planes.

Select a sacred object, a crystal, sigil, written affirmation—and charge it with your intention. Place it somewhere meaningful to you.

Let the physical realm echo your spiritual commitment.

To anchor manifestations, someone can use physical, energetic, or symbolic tools to ground their intention into reality.

Anchoring gives your manifestation a *tangible form* and keeps it energetically "alive" in your environment and subconscious.

Here are powerful ways to do it:

Physical Anchors

These create a *visible or tactile reminder* of your desire:

- **Crystals** (like citrine for abundance or rose quartz for love)
- **Written affirmations or manifestation scripts** are placed where you'll see them often.
- **Vision boards** or manifestation journals.
- **Charm objects or talismans** you can carry or wear!
- **Candles** infused with intention during a ritual (light them regularly to reactivate energy).
- **Photos or symbols** that represent your goal.

Energetic Anchors

These work on a subtle level by *infusing your energy field* with intention:

- **Breathwork patterns** tied to the feeling of your manifestation.
- **Mudras** or hand positions used during meditation.
- **Mantras** or sound vibrations (like chanting "Om Shreem" for prosperity).
- **Essential oils or scents** associated with certain outcomes (e.g., lavender for peace, cinnamon for abundance)
- **Music or frequencies** (like 528 Hz for transformation and miracles)

Ritual or Habitual Anchors

These involve *repeating a sacred practice* that reinforces your intent:

- Lighting a candle each day while visualizing the outcome.

- Touching your anchor object (crystal, amulet) while affirming your desire.
- Setting a daily alarm as a reminder to tune in to your intention.
- Journaling as if the manifestation has already happened.
- Walking meditation or dancing in the energy of what you desire.

Why Anchors Work

Anchors **bridge the gap between thought and form**. They help:

- Keep your vibration aligned with your desire.
- Signal commitment to the Universe.
- Engage your subconscious mind daily.
- Create neural pathways of belief and expectation.

Here are some crystals you could consider using for anchoring your manifest.

🌿 Physical Objects (Talismans & Tools)

Manifestation Type	Suggested Object	Meaning/Purpose
Abundance / Wealth	Citrine crystal, coin, or green aventurine	Amplifies prosperity energy and financial flow
Love / Relationships	Rose quartz, heart-shaped object, or pair of doves	Attracts love, compassion, and connection
Protection / Boundaries	Black tourmaline, evil eye charm, or iron nail	Grounds and protects from negative energy
Health / Vitality	Herbal sachet (e.g. rosemary, eucalyptus) or sun symbol	Encourages healing, strength, and energy
Spiritual Growth / Intuition	Amethyst, owl figurine, or moonstone	Opens third eye, enhances insight and clarity
Success / Career	Key, tiger's eye, or feather	Unlocks opportunities and boosts confidence

Step 7: Release & Trust the Unseen

Let go. Surrender your timeline to divine intelligence. Trust the spiritual currents that carry your desire toward you.

"I release the how. I trust the unfolding."

Psychic Manifesting Journal
A 7-Day Ritual of Energetic Creation

Day 1: The Seed of Intention

Prompt: What do I truly desire right now? Write it as if it already exists.

Psychic Activation: Place your hand on your third eye. Ask: "Show me this reality in spirit."

Affirmation: *"I plant my desire in fertile energy. It already blooms in spirit."*

Day 2: Aligning with Your Desire

Prompt: What beliefs support or block my manifestation?

Activation: Visualize your aura expanding to match your goal's frequency.

Affirmation: *"I match the vibration of my miracle. I align with ease."*

Day 3: Spirit Team Connection

Prompt: Who are my unseen allies? What guidance have they given? Creating a Spirit Team to support you in manifesting is a deeply personal and empowering practice that bridges spiritual connection, intuition, and energetic alignment. Your spirit team is a group of non-physical allies—such as guides, ancestors, angels, spirit animals, higher self, or cosmic beings—who assist you in aligning with your highest potential and intentions.

Activation: Use automatic writing to receive messages.

Affirmation: *"I am guided, supported, and surrounded by loving forces."*

Day 4: Living the Manifestation

Prompt: Describe a day in your manifested life. Living the manifestation means embodying the reality of what you desire—before it physically arrives. This practice transforms you from a passive *wisher* into an active *creator*. The key is to align your thoughts, emotions, energy, and actions with the version of you who already has what you're manifesting.

Activation: Visualize with all senses—add color, sound, movement.

Affirmation: *"My inner world births my outer reality."*

Daily Practice:

- Visualize your life *with* the manifestation.
- Feel it in your body. Smile. Breathe it in.
- Say: *"It is already mine. I am living it now."*

Align your behaviors, choices, and attitude with the version of you who already has it.

Ask:

- What would the successful, healed, or abundant me do today?
- What would I stop tolerating?
- How would I speak, walk, dress, spend time?

Example: Want to manifest love? Start treating yourself how you'd want a partner to treat you.

Old stories, self-doubt, or limiting beliefs will pull you out of alignment. Notice them—not with judgment, but with curiosity.

Ask:

- What thought just contradicted my manifestation?
- Where am I holding resistance?

Then shift:

- Replace it with truth: *"It is safe to receive."*
- Use affirmations, energy clearing, or inner child healing.

Day 5: Physical Anchoring

Prompt: What item or ritual grounds my intention?
Activation: Charge a token with your goal and keep it close.
Affirmation: *"My desire lives in both energy and form."*

Suggestions:

- Sigils or sacred symbols.
- Vision boards.
- Affirmation jars.
- Charged crystals.
- Petition papers under your pillow.

"To manifest is to make the invisible real—but to anchor it, you must give it form. A word spoken, a symbol drawn, a ritual performed—these are the ways spirit settles into matter."

Day 6: Letting Go & Trusting

Prompt: Where am I holding on too tightly?
Activation: Burn or bury written fears. Whisper, *"I release. I trust."*

Affirmation: *"I do not chase—I attract. What is mine flows to me."*

Day 7: Gratitude & Recognition

Prompt: What signs, shifts, or synchronicities have I witnessed?

Activation: Create a "Thank You" ritual. Sing, pray, light incense.

Affirmation: *"Thank you, Universe. I see the magic unfolding."*

Gratitude is the breath that nourishes a manifestation. When you recognize what has arrived—no matter how small—you open the door for more. Every thank you is a signal to the universe: I see, I receive, I honor. In that sacred moment of recognition, your energy aligns with abundance.

Astral Projection

The Soul's Flight Beyond the Body

Astral projection is the conscious separation of your spirit (or astral body) from your physical body, allowing you to explore non-physical realms and dimensions.

How it Feels:

People describe it as floating above their bed, traveling through tunnels of light, or entering dreamlike landscapes. Some meet guides, visit past or future lives, or access spiritual knowledge.

How to Begin:

- Use deep meditation or hypnagogic states (just before sleep).
- Focus on your breath and imagine your energy body lifting.
- Visualize rolling out of your body or climbing a rope upward.
- Set a clear intention to travel safely and return.

As your consciousness separates from the physical body, your energy body vibrates at a higher frequency. This shift often creates distinct physical sensations that can feel surprising or even intense the first few times. These sensations are not distractions—they are milestones of success.

Here is what you may experience:

- **Full-body vibrations**: This is one of the most classic signs that you are entering the astral state. It can feel like being plugged into a current of electricity or like your entire body is humming. These are not physical tremors, they are the subtle body adjusting to higher dimensions.

- **Buzzing or humming sounds**: Some people hear a loud buzzing, ringing, or mechanical sound as the astral body disengages. This sound may rise in intensity and then fade as you shift fully into the non-physical.

- **Pressure or magnetic pulling**: You may feel a tugging or pulling at your head, chest, or solar plexus. This is the energy body gently pulling away from its physical anchor points.

- **Floating, rocking, or swaying**: Even though your physical body is still, your awareness may feel like it is swaying, drifting, or gently floating above the bed or room. You might also feel like you are moving in waves or being lifted.

- **Spinning or falling sensations**: These can feel like being in an elevator that drops or like you are spinning through a vortex. Though disorienting, they signal the loosening of your consciousness from the body.

- **Weightlessness or numbness**: Your body may feel suddenly heavy, then feather-light or even non-existent. This is the release from your physical density.

- **Sudden jolts or jerks (hypnic jerks)**: These can happen right as you are shifting states. While sometimes startling, they are part of the body's natural attempt to "check in" and recalibrate your awareness.

These sensations are often more vivid than any visual, especially in the preliminary stages of practice.

Many beginners become discouraged when they do not "see" an astral world like a movie scene right away. But here is the truth:

You do not need to see to succeed in astral travel—because astral perception is multi-sensory.

You are using a diverse set of "senses" in the astral realm. These include:

- **Clairsentience**: You may feel the presence of people, beings, or places without seeing them. This intuitive feeling often becomes more accurate than vision.

- **Clairaudience**: Some travelers hear guidance, voices, or tones that lead them or deliver messages.

- **Knowing**: You may simply *know* where you are or what is around you without seeing or hearing anything. This is claircognizance.

- **Mental imagery**: Instead of seeing with astral "eyes," you might perceive through inner vision or telepathic download—like receiving information as a clear mental picture or concept.

With time, your astral "sight" will sharpen—but do not wait for it to validate your experience. Trust the energetic sensations; they are the true compass in the non-physical.

What These Sensations Mean

Each sensation is confirmation that your consciousness is detaching from the physical body and tuning into higher frequency realms. The more you lean into these feelings instead of resisting them, the easier and smoother your projection becomes.

Here is a tip:

Do not panic or try to stop the sensations. Fear collapses the projection attempt. Instead, breathe deeply and let yourself flow with the vibration—like surfing a wave.

Practice Tip: Ride the Vibrations

When the energy starts rising and the sensations begin,

1. **Stay calm**. Affirm to yourself: *"This is normal. My soul knows how to travel."*

2. **Focus on lifting out**. Imagine yourself floating, rolling out of your body, or gently rising like mist.

3. **Let the sensations deepen**. They may intensify for 5–30 seconds and then suddenly stop—that is when you are out.

4. **Trust your awareness**. Even if you do not "see," use your mind's eye and emotional radar to explore.

You Are More Than Your Eyes

Your energy body is vast, capable, and ancient. It remembers how to travel the stars. While sight is one tool, your true power lies in your ability to feel, trust, and move through energy with purpose.

If you are vibrating, floating, or sensing presence—you are already astral projecting. The visuals will come, but the sensations are the real doorway.

Astral Projection and **Remote Viewing** are both psychic abilities involving perception beyond the physical senses, but they are quite different in purpose, experience, and technique. Here's a breakdown to help you understand their key differences:

While both astral projection and remote viewing involve expanding your awareness beyond the physical senses, they represent two distinct paths on the psychic journey. Each allows you to explore realms and information beyond your immediate surroundings, but the way you experience and interact with those realms differs. Astral projection feels like a full-bodied journey—your consciousness leaves your physical form to explore other dimensions. In contrast, remote viewing is more like tuning your mind to a distant signal, staying grounded while receiving intuitive impressions. Both abilities tap into the vast potential of human consciousness, yet they serve different purposes and offer unique insights.

Astral Projection

Definition:

Astral projection is the intentional out-of-body experience (OBE) where your consciousness or "astral body" separates from your physical body and explores the astral plane or other dimensions.

Experience:

- Feels like *traveling* outside your body.
- You may see your physical body from above.
- You can visit other realms, meet spirit guides, or explore nonphysical realities.
- The experience can be highly vivid, sensory, and even spiritual.

Purpose:

- Personal exploration
- Spiritual growth
- Healing and guidance
- Connection to higher realms and beings

Indicators:

- Vibrations or buzzing before leaving the body.
- Sensation of floating, flying, or moving through space.
- Awareness of being in another body or environment.

Remote Viewing

Definition:

Remote viewing is the psychic ability to perceive or describe distant or unseen targets (people, places, objects) using only the mind—without physically or astrally traveling there.

Experience:

- Mental impressions or images arrive while you're fully awake and conscious.
- You stay grounded in your body and environment.
- Often practiced with structure or protocols (especially in scientific or military settings).

Purpose:

- Access hidden or distant information.

- Solve problems.
- Locate missing persons/items.
- Investigate timelines or events.

Indicators:

- Subtle visuals, sensations, emotions, or "knowing" about the target.
- Can be verified with real-world data.
- Often works best with focused intention and minimal distractions.

Key Differences:

Aspect	Astral Projection	Remote Viewing
Consciousness	Leaves body (OBE)	Stays in body
Location	Astral realms, nonphysical places	Physical locations in real time (or time travel)

Aspect	Astral Projection	Remote Viewing
Experience	Immersive, like being "there"	Mental, like seeing through the mind's eye
Purpose	Spiritual exploration	Information gathering
Sensory Detail	Full-body sensations, visuals	Abstract impressions, symbols, images

Aura Reading

Interpreting the Soul's Energy Signature

Aura reading is the art of sensing the energetic field surrounding a person, which reflects their emotional, physical, mental, and spiritual state. The aura is an electromagnetic energy field that surrounds every living being. It is constantly shifting in response to thoughts, emotions, health, and spiritual evolution. While some people can see auras with their physical eyes, most experience them through intuitive perception—a blend of feeling, sensing, and inner knowing.

What the Aura Reveals: The Language of Light and Form

Aura reading is not just about seeing pretty colors—it is the art of reading the soul's story through energy. Each aspect of the aura gives you information about a person's well-being, emotions, intentions, and potential.

1. Color Meanings: Emotional, Physical & Spiritual Messages

Each color in the aura reflects a frequency. Here is a detailed guide to what common colors may indicate:

- **Red**: Vitality, passion, courage, physical strength—or, if murky, anger, stress, or overexertion.

- **Orange**: Creativity, joy, sensuality, emotional openness—or imbalance in relationships if cloudy.

- **Yellow**: Intelligence, optimism, confidence, personal power—or anxiety or overthinking if dull.

- **Green**: Healing energy, love, compassion, balance—or jealousy or emotional suppression if darkened.

- **Blue**: Communication, peace, spiritual truth, empathy, or a need to express oneself more clearly.

- **Indigo**: Intuition, insight, spiritual awareness, psychic abilities—or detachment, if it seems faded.

- **Violet**: Enlightenment, divine connection, transformation—or escapism if too etheric or unstable.

- **White**: Purity, high spiritual frequency, protection, alignment with higher self.

- **Black or gray patches**: Energy blockages, grief, illness, spiritual stagnation—these areas need clearing, not fear.

Color is contextual and may change moment to moment depending on mood, health, or environment. Trust your first impression—how the color feels to you is as important as any chart.

2. Shapes, Density, and Fluctuations: The Architecture of Energy

- **Spiky or jagged edges**: Defensiveness, unresolved trauma, psychic overload.

- **Smooth, rounded aura**: Emotional balance, strong boundaries, peaceful presence.

- **Dense or thick aura**: Groundedness, strong physical vitality—or possibly emotional rigidity.

- **Thin or faded aura**: Fatigue, depletion, depression, or a sensitive/empathic nature absorbing too much from others.

- **Swirling or dancing movements**: Creative energy, rapid emotional shifts, psychic sensitivity.

- **Dark spots or holes**: Indicate areas where energy is leaking or blocked—often related to trauma or illness.

These subtle patterns tell a story of the person's inner life and can guide healing, emotional understanding, and intuitive development.

3. Sensing the Aura Without Sight

You do *not* need to "see" auras to read them effectively. Many powerful aura readers are clairsentient (they *feel* energy). Here are common sensations:

- **Heat or warmth**: Strong life force, emotional intensity, or healing energy.

- **Coolness or chill**: Spiritual presence, calm detachment, or possible energetic depletion.

- **Tingling or buzzing**: Activation of spiritual gifts, presence of guides, or incoming messages.

- **Pressure or heaviness**: Unprocessed emotion, stress, spiritual resistance.

- **Emotional mirroring**: You may feel another person's mood in your own body—this is empathic aura sensing.

The more you practice, the more your sensitivity grows.

Practicing Aura Reading: How to Activate Your Inner Sight

Aura reading is a skill, not a talent. Here is a more detailed step-by-step approach to help you begin and strengthen your ability.

Step 1: Sense Your Own Aura

1. **Activate Your Hands**:
   Rub your palms together until you feel warmth and energy. This awakens the energy centers in your hands.

2. **Feel the Space Between**:
   Slowly separate your hands and bring them close again, about 3–6 inches apart. You may feel resistance, magnetism, or a tingling field. This is your auric energy.

3. **Scan Your Body**:
   Move your hands around your body slowly, a few inches away from your skin. Notice if the sensations change—heat, coolness, resistance, or "holes" in the field may appear.

4. **Journal Your Experience**:

    Record your impressions. What did you feel? Did images or colors come to mind?

Step 2: See the Aura Around Another Person

1. **Choose the Right Setting**:

    Ask a friend to stand about 4–6 feet away from you, in front of a plain white or light-colored wall. Natural lighting works best.

2. **Soften Your Gaze**:

    Look at the space just beyond their body, especially around the head and shoulders. Let your vision blur slightly. Do not stare too hard.

3. **Watch for Flickers or Haze**:

    A glow, mist, or color may begin to appear. Often, you will first see a white or pale blue outline, which may deepen into stronger colors with time.

4. **Validate with Intuition**:

    Even if you do not "see" the aura, tune into your feelings. What do you sense emotionally or energetically when near them? Your intuitive response is part of the aura reading.

Practice Tip: Mirror Work

Practice in the mirror. Stand in front of a white background and look gently past your own shoulder. Be patient, trust the process. Many see their first aura after several short sessions.

Final Words: Reading Auras with Heart and Intuition

Aura reading is an intuitive art, not a science. While charts and meanings provide guidance, the *real magic* comes when you begin trusting your inner sense of what you are receiving.

The aura is your soul's song in color and vibration. When you read someone's aura, you are not just seeing their energy, you are witnessing their truth, pain, and potential.

Treat it with reverence.

The Psychic Mindset

What You Need to Know to Begin to See Auras:

Before stepping into any of these arts, here are five essential truths to guide your journey:

1. You Already Have the Gift.
   Everyone is born psychic—it is just a matter of remembering and refining.

2. Energy is Real—Even If You Cannot See It Yet.
   Just as you do not see Wi-Fi but benefit from it, energy flows through everything. Your intention and attention are enough to start tuning in.

3. Belief Opens the Door. Doubt Slams It Shut.
   Suspend disbelief. Approach these practices with curiosity, not skepticism.

4. Stillness is Your Portal.
   Psychic information comes best when your mind is quiet. Meditation, breathwork, and mindfulness sharpen your inner senses.

5. Spiritual Ethics Matter.
   Always approach these abilities with respect, integrity, and love. Never use them to control or manipulate. Your power is sacred.

You are not just a seeker of mystery; you are made of mystery.
Your soul remembers how to travel, to see, to know.

Remote viewing, astral projection, and aura reading are not far-off powers—they are soul skills awaiting your remembrance.

Trust the Journey Within

As we come to the close of this chapter in your psychic journey, remember this: psychic abilities are not a mysterious gift reserved for the chosen few—they are a natural extension of your intuition, a sixth sense that everyone possesses in some form. You have already taken the key step by exploring, questioning, and awakening your inner knowing.

Whether your psychic connection feels like a whisper on the breeze or a thunderclap of certainty, trust that it is real. Trust that it is yours.

Your abilities may come naturally, or they may unfold with study, practice, and patience—just like building a muscle, learning a language, or fine-tuning a musical instrument. You are not alone in this path. You are part of a long lineage of seekers, sensitives, and explorers who have dared to go beyond the veil of the ordinary in search of deeper truth.

Know that even the most advanced psychic practices—like remote viewing or astral projection—are within your reach when paired with dedication, meditation, and belief in your own potential. Like an athlete honing their skills until movement becomes instinctive, your psychic senses can become trusted allies that respond without hesitation.

Conclusion

The Beginning of Your Psychic Journey

As we close the closing chapter of *Your Psychic Connection*, we return to the heart of this book's purpose—an invitation to *awaken, explore, and trust* your innate psychic abilities. This journey is not only about developing intuition or experiencing paranormal phenomena; it is about transforming your understanding of yourself and the universe. Whether you came to this book out of curiosity, skepticism, or the pull of the unknown, you now hold in your hands a key—one that unlocks the doors to both scientific inquiry and metaphysical exploration.

Your Psychic Connection is rooted in a simple yet profound truth: *we all have the ability to connect beyond the five senses.* Through guided exercises, reflective journaling, and a blend of personal experience and parapsychological insights, this book has offered tools to help you discover the psychic power within.

Now, we challenge you to go deeper.

Your Dual Challenge: Scientific & Metaphysical

- **Scientific Challenge**: Begin documenting your psychic experiences using a structured approach. Record your dreams, premonitions, intuitive hits, and any paranormal encounters. Use your journal as data—track patterns, synchronicities, and verifiable outcomes. Treat your psychic development as a study of the unseen, applying logic, reason, and empirical analysis. Can you validate your intuition through real-world evidence?

- **Metaphysical Challenge**: Choose one psychic ability—clairvoyance, telepathy, psychometry, or mediumship—and immerse yourself in its practice for 30 days. Meditate daily, ground your energy, and engage with higher vibrations. Call on your spirit guides, trust your impressions, and surrender to the unknown. Ask yourself: *What truths does the universe wish to reveal to me?*

As you continue this path, know that you are not alone. The Family Spirit Supernatural team walks with you, offering guidance through our other powerful books, including:

- **Parapsychology 101 Your Journey of the Unexplained**—A comprehensive guide to the scientific study of the parapsychology. The book includes tools and stories to illuminate your spiritual awakening.

- **Tales in the Dark**—Campfire stories from the turn of the century written in a manner to help you retale the stories with your family and friends.

- **So, You Think Your Kid is Psychic?**—A parent's guide to nurturing intuitive children.

- **Haunted Countryside**—A gently haunted story for children about siblings from America's heartland.

- **Family Spirit Five Generations of the Supernatural**—Our own legacy of five generations in the supernatural–A deep dive into our family's haunted lineage.

- **Haunted Objects: Possessions That Refuse to Die**—The chilling truth behind cursed artifacts, haunted objects and the energy they carry.

The journey does not end here—it evolves. Follow the trail of truth, fear, wonder, and wisdom through the eyes of our family and fellow investigators.

You have seen us share these stories and experiences on your favorite paranormal shows.

- **Leitreanna Brown** on *My Ghost Story: Caught on Camera* (A&E/Bio), *Haunted Hospitals* (Travel Channel/Destination America), and *Repossessed* (History Channel/Hulu/Apple TV/Disney+/Discovery+)

- **Matthew Brown** on *Paranormal Witness* (Syfy)

- **Matthew & Leitreanna Brown**, alongside **Judy Terry**, on *Family Spirits* (HauntTV, T&E, PlutoTV, Plex, and Xumo Play).

- **Matthew & Leitreanna Brown** on *24 Hours in Hell: The Waldorf Estate* (Network to be announced).

Each appearance offers a glimpse into the reality behind the veil—confirming that the supernatural is not only real, but also deeply personal. **As you close this book, know that you are not at the end**—you are just beginning.

Your Psychic Connection was created to be more than just a guide; it is also a journal, a companion, and a sacred space for you to explore your inner world. Within these pages, you've been given tools to awaken your intuition, exercises to stretch your psychic senses, and space to reflect, record, and rediscover your soul's wisdom.

Whether you've felt tingles in your palms, glimpses of color in someone's aura, vivid dreams that left a message, or simply a stronger sense of "knowing" in your day-to-day life, you are reconnecting—with your spirit, your gifts, and your greater purpose.

Trust the journey. Some days, the path will feel bright and affirming. Other days, it may feel quiet or uncertain. Both are part of the process. Your psychic connection is a living energy—it expands the more you listen, the more you practice, and the more you trust what arises from within.

This book is here for you whenever you need to return to it. Use it repeatedly as your abilities deepen. Let it hold your evolving insights, dreams, and awakenings.

And remember, this is only the beginning.

Your abilities can take you further than you ever imagined—into realms of healing, energy work, remote perception, even co-creating your reality with the Universe itself. In the next volume, we'll go deeper into those very frontiers: manifesting with psychic intention, soul-level energy alignment, and walking the path of the mystic in everyday life.

Until then, keep journaling. Keep sensing. Keep trusting.

You were born with this light.

Now you are learning to shine it.

Made in the USA
Columbia, SC
08 July 2025